MORE THAN JUST A SHOP

The History of the Co-op in Lancashire

MORE THAN JUST A SHOP

The History of the Co-op in Lancashire

Jean Turnbull and Jayne Southern

Lancashire County Books, 1995

More than just a shop: the history of the Co-op in Lancashire
by Jean Turnbull and Jayne Southern

Published by Lancashire County Books, 1995

Typeset in Monotype Baskerville by Carnegie Publishing Ltd, 18 Maynard St, Preston, Lancs.
Printed and bound in the UK by Redwood Books, Trowbridge

British Library Cataloguing in Publication Data
A CIP record for this book is available from the British Library

ISBN 1-871236-36-3

Lancashire County Books is part of Lancashire County Library Service and has as its remit the publication of books and pamphlets with academic and general appeal dealing with all aspects of the history of the county.

The Historical Association (founded 1906) is a national organisation with branches throughout the country. It provides a range of activities and publications at national and local level for people who share an interest in, and love for, the past. Further details can be obtained from the Historical Association, 59a Kennington Park Road, London SE11 4JH.

The two organisations have collaborated to further these aims and to produce a series of high quality, illustrated pamphlets and short booklets written by acknowledged experts in their fields, designed to bring some of the fruits of recent scholarship to a wide audience.

Already published in this series:
John K. Walton, *Wonderlands by the Waves: a History of the Seaside Resorts of Lancashire* (1992)
Jeffrey Richards, *Stars in Our Eyes: Lancashire Stars of Stage, Screen and Radio* (1994)
Robert Poole, *The Lancashire Wakes Holidays* (1994)

In preparation:
Michael Winstanley (ed.), *Working Children in Nineteenth-Century Lancashire*

Foreword

Everybody born before the 1960s seems to remember their family's 'divi' number which entitled them to share in the profits of their local co-operative society, but not everybody is aware that the Co-op was and is much more than just a shop. In terms of business it has long been involved in wholesale, production, banking and insurance and it still undertakes extensive political, educational and cultural activities. In this booklet we aim to trace the development of the Co-op and these associated activities in Lancashire and to assess the way in which co-operation in the county reflected national trends, looking at its growth, heyday and the way it has to adapt to changing circumstances, especially since the 1960s, while holding on to the ideals which have always been an integral part of the movement.

An early photograph in the Rochdale area, the 'home' of the Co-operative movement, in the days before shop fronts *(Co-operative Union)*.

The Co-op as a Business

Origins and Early Development

The Co-operative movement had its origins in the 1820s and 1830s as part of a wider socialist vision. Its supporters, inspired by Robert Owen, advocated the creation of co-operative communities in which members would have an equal share in the ownership and control of land, food and industrial production, and distribution. Owen helped to found Co-operative communities, like New Harmony in America, and was associated subsequently with Queenswood in England, which were to further the cause. Large numbers of small societies were founded during this period to supply goods to members and raise funds for the movement. In this first phase of co-operative development, Lancashire, together with the West Riding of Yorkshire and London and Brighton, would appear to have been the main areas of activity. By the early 1830s there were eleven societies in the vicinity of Manchester and nine in the Bolton area and societies temporarily appeared in other parts of the county, including Liverpool (1829), Wigan (1833) and Lancaster (1836). These were supported by regional conferences, journals and local meetings, and Lancashire played an important role in these from the outset as well. For example, Manchester hosted the first ever co-operative conference in 1831, at which fifty-six societies and a total membership in excess of three thousand were represented, and five out of the seven subsequent conferences were held in either Lancashire or Yorkshire. Co-operative newspapers were published including the *United Trades Co-operative Journal* (Manchester) and *The Lancashire Co-operator*, published in Liverpool in 1830, whilst a co-operative wholesale company was also set up in Liverpool, in 1831.

However, this early flourish was short-lived, with the onset of depression in 1834 and the collapse of the Chartist and trade union movements resulting in the closure of many societies, including many of those in Lancashire. When the economy recovered in the mid-1840s emphasis shifted from idealism to pragmatism, with the earlier visions of utopian communities tempered by a greater emphasis on retailing. This form of co-operation was most associated with the weavers of Rochdale, soon christened the 'Rochdale Pioneers', who set up a store in 1844. The basis of this and subsequent retail co-operative societies was the voluntary coming together of working-class people to establish a shop through the issue of shares. In all cases members owned the enterprise, assisted in the management, shared in the profits, and were represented by a management committee, which was democratically elected at quarterly and half-yearly meetings. The rules of the Rochdale Pioneers laid down a set of principles, which included a commitment to providing pure, unadulterated food; an insistence upon cash payment for goods; dividends on purchases; and democratic control. They also put aside 2½ per cent of profits for educational purposes and remained true to the long term realisation of the wider ideals of founding the Co-operative Commonwealth through gradual change. Its original principles committed it to

> the establishment of a store for the sale of provisions, clothing, etc.
>
> the building, purchasing, or erecting of a number of houses, in which those members desiring to assist each other in improving their domestic and social conditions may reside.
>
> . . . the manufacture of such articles as the society may determine upon for the employment of such members as may be without employment or who may be suffering in consequence of repeated reduction in their wages.
>
> . . . purchase or rent an estate or estates of land, which shall be cultivated by members who may be out of employment or whose labour may be badly remunerated.

In addition it was intended that

> as soon as practicable, this society shall proceed to arrange the powers of production, distribution, education and government; or in other words to establish a self-supporting colony of united interests or assist other societies in establishing such colonies.
>
> for the promotion of sobriety a temperance hotel be opened in one of the society's houses as soon as convenient.

These principles, therefore, reflected many of the ideals of earlier societies, representing an egalitarian and democratic attempt to improve the living standards and intellectual horizons of the working classes. What was

Some of the co-ops issued lightweight metal (later plastic) tokens when goods were bought. The Rochdale Provident Co-operative Society issued a wide range of values of token in both penny and shilling denominations. The smaller values could be exchanged for larger ones. The £1 token here is from Ingleton Industrial Co-operative. In some areas tokens and paper 'divi' chits ran side by side. Plastic tokens were later used in some societies to buy bread and milk from the delivery vans to save drivers handling cash. Some modern societies have reintroduced tokens for milk deliveries *(Lancashire Library Local Studies Collection from material supplied by the Co-operative Union).*

important was the introduction of the dividend on purchases, paid to members of the society in proportion to the amount they spent in the store, which put the Co-operative movement on to a more secure and efficient financial footing. It was the 'divi', as it soon became known, which was to prove to be one of the most popular features of co-operative societies for well over a century.

The most usual way of receiving a record of money spent was a chitty of paper for each transaction. Copies of each chitty were collected centrally and totalled each quarter so that the dividend could be paid to each customer. The above photograph shows the laborious process of collecting the chits and the one opposite shows customers standing in line to collect their 'divi' *(Co-operative Union)*.

Every member was given a unique number when they joined. Each time they made a purchase at the stores their membership number was noted down, together with the total price paid for the goods. By this process the society had a record of the amount of money spent by each member and thus was able to calculate their dividend as a proportion of their purchases. Dividends were set and paid quarterly, and rose to as much as three or four shillings in the pound in the more successful societies in the early twentieth century when the movement exhibited its greatest expansion. Members queued on dividend day, often for several hours, to collect their money. The system was believed to encourage thrift, as it was one of few forms of saving open to ordinary working-class people and these relatively large sums were frequently earmarked for the purchase of children's clothing and other expensive family items, or for the annual holiday in Wakes Week.

The principles adopted by the Rochdale Pioneers were widely promoted through publications and the work of 'missionaries' and soon became the model for all subsequent societies which were formed as prosperity in the textile districts grew from mid-century. Thirty-nine new societies were founded between 1844 and 1853 and approximately 350 societies in the following decade. For the most part the earliest societies were located in the industrialised south-east portion of the county, many in the Pennine area close to the boundary with Yorkshire. These included Bacup (1850), Stacksteads and Oldham Industrial (1851), Littleborough (1853), Firgrove (1854), Mossley (1856), Oldham Equitable, Heale, Eccles and Royton (1857), Whitworth and Middleton & Tonge (1957), Ramsbottom and Westhoughton Friendly (1858), Failsworth, Bolton, Manchester & Salford and Stalybridge (1959). By the 1860s the movement was spreading to other parts of the county, including north Lancashire, for example Lancaster & Skerton, Nelson, Darwen, and Barrow-in-Furness (1860); Bamber Bridge, Clitheroe, Swarthmoor & Ulverston and Dalton-in-Furness (1861). By 1870, there were 112 societies, approximately one quarter of the total in England and many of these continued to operate well into the twentieth century.

With the revival of the movement after 1844 new organisations appeared to service it and, given the early importance of the textile districts, Manchester rapidly emerged as the natural centre to house these agencies. These included: the North of England Wholesale Agency and Depot Society Ltd, (later the Co-operative Wholesale Society or CWS), which was set up in 1863 to supply goods to affiliated societies; the Co-operative Insurance Company (1867) and

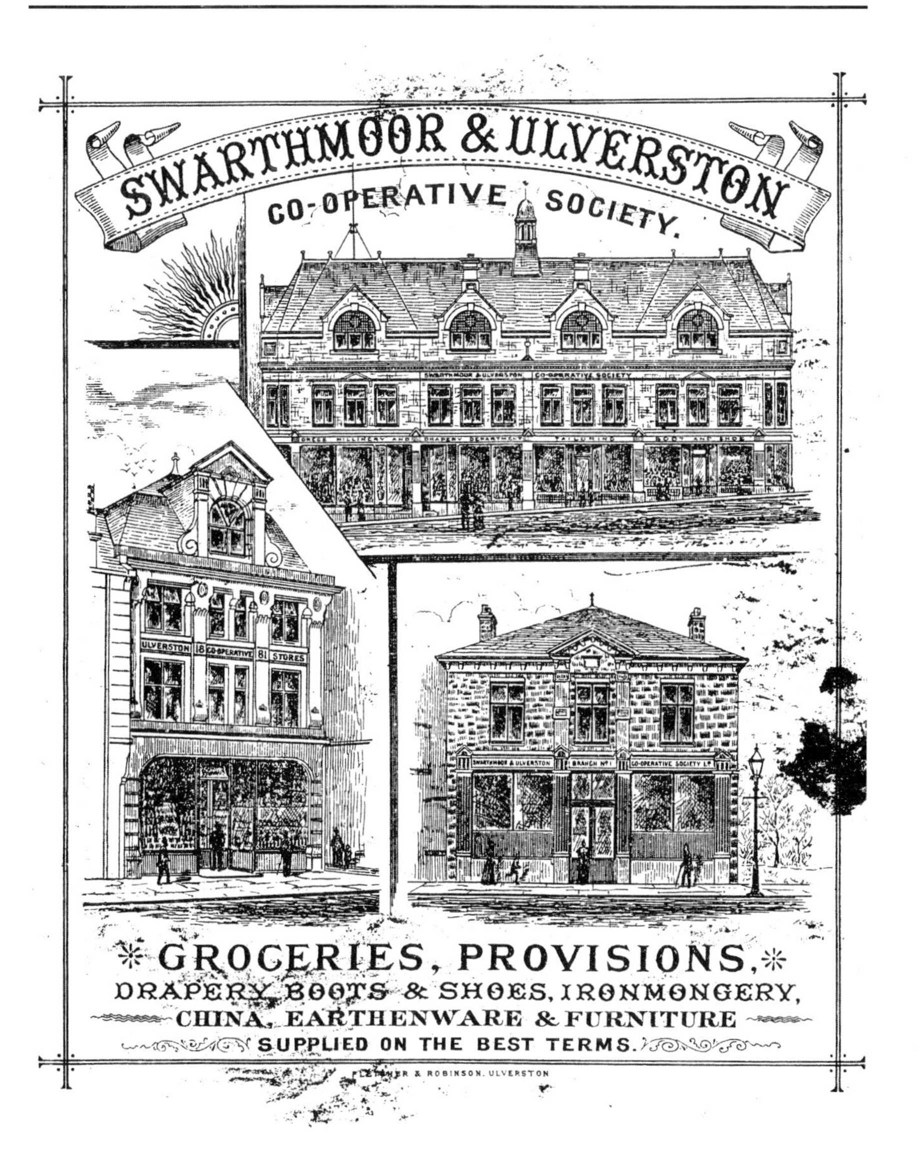

Shop front designs for branches of the Swarthmoor and Ulverston Co-operative Society *(Jean Turnbull)*.

A Christmas card of the Dalton-in-Furness central premises *(Jean Turnbull)*.

the Central Board of Co-operation (later the Co-operative Union) in 1871. The Co-operative Press, which published the movement's main newspapers, *The Co-operative News* and *The Wheatsheaf*, amongst its many other publications and, somewhat later, the Co-operative Bank, were also both located in the city of Manchester. The buildings erected by these organisations dominated – and indeed still dominate – a whole section of the city.

One of the main objectives of the CWS was to provide societies with goods produced in co-operative factories and workshops, which could be guaranteed to have been produced under trade union pay and conditions. In this area Lancashire also played an important role, with a heavy concentration of CWS production centred in the Manchester area. The first CWS factory, in Lower Crumpsall near Manchester in 1873, produced biscuits and sweets, and other ventures which were subsequently established included the Irlam Soap, Candle, Lard and Starch Works; Manchester Tobacco, Cigar, Cigarette and

Housewives were encouraged to purchase goods made in the co-operative factories and workshops. The above photograph shows the Margarine and Lard Works in Irlam *(Co-operative Union)*.

Snuff Works; Rochdale Paint, Varnish and Colour Works, and a number of very large flour and provender mills in the Manchester and Oldham areas. Finally, in keeping with the tradition of textile Lancashire, the CWS opened weaving sheds in Bury (1905) and Radcliffe (1913), producing sheets and blankets, amongst other goods.

The Central Board of Co-operation and the Co-operative Union sought to encourage individual societies to participate in the aims and objectives of the wider movement. To this effect it divided the country into 'sections' in 1873 with District Boards and conferences to enable better communication between the central headquarters and local societies. One of the Co-op Union's main objectives was to exhort both societies and their membership to greater loyalty and solidarity. Societies were encouraged at conference

Two advertisements from the Chorley Co-operative Society *Monthly Record* May 1900 illustrating support for own brands and for buying goods produced in collieries whose methods were in line with the movement's ideas *(Lancashire County Library, Chorley Local Studies Collection)*.

meetings to buy produce from the CWS and to subordinate their own society interests to those of the wider movement, whilst members were urged to be more loyal to their own society. To help sustain expansion, the Co-op Union was also active in the formation of societies in areas where few societies existed – known as 'co-operative wildernesses'.

The last quarter of the nineteenth century saw a dramatic rise in working-class living standards which led to a range of new retail organisations appearing in Britain, including department and multiple stores. Not surprisingly, this also affected the Co-operative movement. Nationally, there was a sustained rise in the number of societies, especially after 1880, so that by 1899 1,500 retail co-operative societies were in existence. Whereas only 1 per cent of the population were members in the early 1870s, over 4 per cent had joined by 1900 and sales accounted for an estimated 6 per cent of the country's retail trade, rising to an estimated 7–9 per cent by 1920. In Lancashire, the number and size of the societies also rose dramatically. Societies founded between 1870 and 1879 included: Colne & District (1870), Preston (1873), Longridge (1874), Leyland & Farington (1875) and Ribchester (1876) so that by 1879 there were 180 societies. Thereafter the foundation of the Fleetwood (1880) and Blackpool (1885) societies owed much to the efforts of the Co-operative Union while growth was also evident in Merseyside bringing the total number to 200 by 1899. Membership in the county rose from just 150,000 in 1879 to over half a million by 1914 and in many communities the level was such that practically all families had at least one member in the local society. Growth continued through the First World War, despite adverse trading conditions, with national membership increasing from three million in 1914 to over four million in 1919. However, because of the movement's expansion elsewhere in the country, Lancashire was no longer as dominant as it had been in the early years.

After 1900 the trend in Lancashire, as elsewhere in the country, was also towards amalgamation into fewer societies and by 1914 the number had been marginally reduced to 181. This and the growth in membership meant that the average society increased from 1,024 members in 1884 to 3,037 in 1914, although this figure disguised the great variations in size. In 1914 four societies had fewer than 100 members with White Coppice (Bolton District) the smallest society with only twenty-three members and Salterforth (North East Lancashire District) with just sixty-nine members. Eighty-three societies had in excess of 1,000 members, whilst sixteen had membership which

An example of a general grocery store with separate but adjoinng butchery department in Eldon Street, Preston *(Preston: a handbook to the thirty-ninth annual Co-operative Congress, Whitsuntide 1907 [CWS, 1907], p. 95).*

exceeded 10,000, the two largest societies being Bolton and Pendleton (Manchester), the former with over 38,000 members, the latter with over 29,000 members.

As membership grew, and the CWS expanded its operations, the range of goods which societies sold also expanded. Most co-operative societies initially began by selling basic provisions; by the 1880s the Co-operative Directories show that they were selling all manner of goods: groceries, drapery, hardware, boots and shoes, furnishings, ironmongery and coal. Many societies also had butchery, tailoring, clogging and bakery departments. By this date even relatively small one-store societies had diversified their trade with, for example, Kirkby-in-Furness having separate grocery, butchery and boot and shoe departments, whilst Grange-over-Sands sold groceries, boots and shoes, coal and earthenware and had a separate tailoring department. In order to accommodate the growing range of goods and services, societies were obliged to move out of their initial premises, opening branches as new areas were colonised and building impressive new town-centre premises which were a physical manifestation of their confidence and prosperity. The period before the First World war with rising membership, expanding trade and high dividends was one of optimism and pride, and this was reflected in the jubilee histories of many societies which were written in the years between 1894 to 1914. These were published by most – but not all – of the Lancashire societies and provide a record of their early history, their foundation, progress and membership.

Adaptation and Decline

Although membership of co-operative societies continued to increase in the inter-war years, there were signs that the movement was beginning to lose momentum. The social background of members in a society generally reflected the dominant industry of an area: iron ore miners and later shipbuilders were the backbone of societies in Furness like the Dalton-in-Furness and Swarthmoor & Ulverston societies; coal and heavy industrial communities were also important in southern central Lancashire while textile workers supported those in east Lancashire. The decline of many of these industries during the inter-war years, combined with further expansion in the South and Midlands undermined the relative importance of Lancashire in the Co-operative movement. Within the county, too, the heartland of textile Lancashire was eclipsed by growth in other areas, especially Merseyside, in the specific new industrial developments around the Manchester Ship Canal and Trafford Park, and in the towns of Preston and Lancaster and those along the Fylde coast, all of which reflected the different economic fortunes of the region.

The stagnant trading performance of the cotton districts can also be attributed to the fact that the Co-op had already reached saturation point; because most local people were already enrolled, it was hard to expand either by attracting new members or by encouraging existing members to spend more. Furthermore, despite some pre-war amalgamations there was still a large number of small co-ops which meant that it was difficult for any of them to expand their operations geographically without coming into conflict with

In 1890 Preston had 'excellent up-to-date abattoirs and a bakery, with stabling and other conveniences' which were situated in Moor Lane and at that time 'considered to be the best of their kind in the Kingdom' *(Memento of the Guild Merchant, 1902 [CWS, 1902], p. 71).*

neighbouring societies. The Co-op Union was consistently in favour of the amalgamation of neighbouring co-ops to curb this potentially damaging competition and the disputes about boundaries between societies, and to improve business efficiency and competitiveness against other retail organisations. Its campaign was stepped up during the 1920s and 1930s with some success; 1932 saw the amalgamation of the Blackburn and Blackburn Livesey societies in the North-East Lancashire district, whilst, in the same year in the Rossendale District, Helmshore was taken over by Haslingden. But those amalgamations which did occur were often the result of one of the participating societies getting into financial difficulties. In these situations, an amalgamation was, in effect, a take-over. This was certainly the case when the more prosperous Carnforth Society was amalgamated with Grange-over-Sands as early as 1904 and when the successful Swarthmoor & Ulverston Society amalgamated with Penny Bridge in 1901. But the county continued to contain some of the smallest co-ops in the country with, for example, attempts to weld the nine Manchester societies into one coming to nothing. Its best efforts were often frustrated as many retail societies' management committees continued to exhibit fierce local pride and disagreed with the central initiatives of the movement, believing that they reduced local autonomy and ordinary member participation.

To increase trade and membership, therefore, a policy of 'intensive' trading was also favoured which involved further diversification into new areas, providing milk and coal deliveries, hairdressing salons and funeral parlours. Some societies were obliged to combine to provide these services. The Accrington & Church, Oswaldtwistle and Burnley societies, for example, formed a Federal Dairy in 1931; the 3Es Bakery was set up by the Eagley, Egerton and Edgworth societies; a North-East Lancashire Co-operative Laundries Association was formed in 1934 and the Merseyside and District Funeral Services in 1939. This period also saw the beginnings of a new phenomenon, the travelling shop, a development which was to expand dramatically in the years following the Second World War. However, not all societies in Lancashire could afford to be so progressive, because small co-ops, like those in the Rossendale district, simply lacked the resources to invest in new departments and services.

During the Second World War the movement had to confront additional problems related to licensing for raw materials, price controls and rationing. It also had to cope with the secondment of its staff, the loss of customers due to mass evacuation, and the damage and disruption caused by bombing, air raids and black-outs with the premises of many co-operative societies in large

216
M&S
CO-OPERATIVE
RNB 616

M&S
BREAD
SERVICE
CO-OPERATIVE

OLDHAM INDUSTRIAL PASTEURISED MILK AND CREAM

is good for you!

Home delivery was a standard service provided by shopkeepers and the co-op was no exception. Seen here are (opposite, top) an early horse-drawn bread wagon, (opposite, bottom) a 1950s electric milk float of the Manchester and Salford Society *(Co-operative Union)* and (above) a lorry and tricycles used to deliver milk in the Oldham area (The Wheatsheaf, *June 1936).*

cities and ports receiving direct hits. Sales of both foodstuffs and dry goods rose in monetary value but the actual volume of trade was lower in 1945 than in 1939. But in some respects the war also helped the movement and allowed it to increase its percentage share of national trade. This was due to a number of factors, especially the Co-op's reliance on basic commodities rather than luxury items and the undisputed attraction of dividend on purchases due to the standardisation of prices. Since co-ops sometimes had trouble in meeting the demands of their members for certain goods like jam, because under the points system of rationing the supply of goods to shops was dependent upon their pre-war level of sales, they increasingly turned to the CWS for their supplies, strengthening co-ordination between different levels of the movement. This was also helped by the Agricultural and Marketing Department of the Co-operative Union and the co-operative trade associations, which represented consumer interests on official government committees and by the Co-op Union's advice to local societies, through the issuing of special 'War Emergency Circulars' to explain the mounting number of war-time rules and regulations governing retail trade.

The movement, therefore, seemed well placed after the war had ended and initially continued to prosper through the 1950s as consumer expenditure rose. From the 1960s, however, with changes in spending habits and the nature of retailing, including increasing price competition from multiples and chain stores, the movement began to encounter difficulties leading to a fall in its membership and a deteriorating trading performance. In 1969 Lancastria Co-op replaced cash dividends with trading stamps for all its customers regardless of membership. This was in line with general trends, as the old system had become increasingly expensive to operate for the increasingly small dividends and was largely killed off by the conversion to decimal currency in 1971. Growing price competition and lower profit margins led to the abandonment of stamps in 1982. This has altered the financial base of societies, forcing them to increase their reserves to become less dependent upon members' share capital, since the loss of the dividend meant there was less financial incentive to become a member of the movement. More recently, competition has been intensified by late-night and Sunday shopping and the invasion of foreign discount stores. National membership figures, which had risen from over 10 million in 1948 to almost 13 million in 1968, disguised the fact that those in some areas, including the north-west, were declining. From the late 1960s the decline became national. All this has meant that there has

An advertisement from *The Wheatsheaf* during the Second World War in which the important role of the women in Lancashire in peacetime and in the war is extolled (November 1941).

Promoting its own products in another wartime issue of *The Wheatsheaf*. Each of the biscuits shows where it was made (February 1942).

been a significant drop in the Co-op's share of total retail trade. In the early 1950s it represented 10 per cent of national sales as opposed to 20 per cent for the multiples; in the early 1960s the Co-op's market share peaked at 12 per cent, but by April 1994 it was only 4 per cent. Similarly, the movement's share of the total grocery trade has shrunk from 20 per cent in the early 1950s to 7.2 per cent in April 1994. At 1.4 per cent the current figure for dry goods demonstrates a long-standing weakness. However, the Co-op accounts for a quarter of all the nation's funeral business, which is a much more impressive market penetration. Nevertheless, although some areas in the south and midlands have continued to grow others, including the north-west, have encountered difficulties, so that today the Co-op no longer has stores in every town.

In many ways the Co-op's democratic and federal structure did not lend itself to adapt easily to the rigours of the modern post-war world. Its federal organisation continued to result in uneven geographical provision of goods and services and reduced the ability to take uniform and sustained action to invest in and modernise shops and products. The movement was well aware, however, that changes in retailing and increased competition coupled with its own continuing internal weaknesses were damaging its long-term prospects and efforts were intensified to reform and rationalise both the constitution and business enterprises. Again the key themes were centralisation, amalgamation and specialisation and these were the watchwords of the main vehicle of reform, namely the Independent Commission of Inquiry, which was set up in 1955 and reported in 1958. It approved the abolition of the old Central Board whch had taken place in 1952, but recommended that the Sectional Boards, including the North West, be more closely informed about all national committees. As part of the amalgamation policy a survey was conducted by the new Central Executive and published in 1960 taking the idea of amalgamation one step further and considering the welding together of all the societies in one area into one super co-op. As a result of this, the number of societies nationally fell dramatically from 467 in 1967 to 312 in 1976 and only 55 societies in 1994.

The story of the Co-operative Wholesale Society (CWS) has been equally chequered, reflecting increasing competition and the fluctuating fortunes of the retail societies. It underwent major constitutional reform in 1965 and two years later it spear-headed a marketing campaign to establish firmer relations between itself and the retail societies and to create a more standardised image in what became known as 'Operation Facelift'. The years since 1958, however,

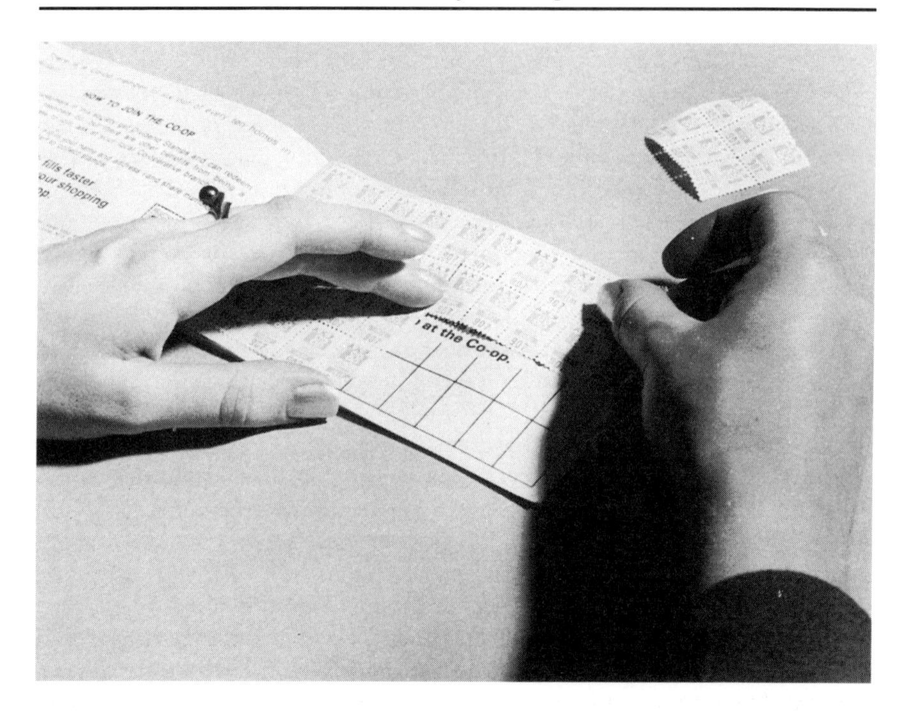

Trading stamps were very popular in the 1970s and the Co-op issued its own stamps with the motto 'the stamps you can shop with'. Each page took forty stamps and there were three values; the single, a five stamp and a forty stamp. A full book of thirty pages could be redeemed for cash, for goods or paid into a share account *(Co-operative Union)*.

have seen the rationalisation, reduction and final abandonment of production by the CWS, which today has become one of the biggest retail co-operatives in its own right. There have, therefore, also been attempts to merge the major central institutions of the Co-op, such as the CWS, the Scottish Co-operative Wholesale Society, the Co-operative Productive Federation and the Co-operative Union, into one national organisation but, as in the past, not all co-operators believe that big is beautiful.

In terms of the north-west, these central reforms of the Co-op, especially the amalgamation programme, have had a great impact. In 1945 232 societies were to be found in the North Western Section; in 1955 there were 193; ten years later the number was down to 122, and by 1975 there were only 39. Today only a few very small independent societies, such as Coniston and Hawkshead, still remain in existence, the Co-operative Retail Services Ltd (CRS) covers the north-east of the county and Merseyside, while most of Lancashire is catered for by one huge co-op called the United Norwest.

United Norwest is the product of a number of earlier amalgamations within the region which had experienced mixed fortunes (see Appendix). Lancastria Co-op, for example, was formed in 1968 and proved to be a progressive and financially sound society, as it quadrupled its money sales and almost doubled its sales in real terms by 1975. When it was merged into the Greater Lancastria Co-op in 1976, *The Co-operative News* reported that it had a membership of 30,000 served by 4,000 employees and generated an annual sales turnover of £61 million. Its trading area covered over 3,000 square miles and from its main headquarters in Blackpool it operated over 300 supermarkets and retail outlets, including a wide range of dry goods and services, such as department stores in all major towns, chemists, hairdressers, petrol stations and travel bureaux. It also undertook large projects at Preston and Hindley, but the 'Pricefighters' were its main development and by 1982 it had twenty-one of these stores, which aimed to replace dividend stamps with a 5 per cent discount. In contrast to the successful Lancastria, however, Greater Lancastria proved to be a loss-maker, as its figures slid, then rallied, before settling into a downward trend which by 1982 had reduced the value of the society's sales almost back to the smaller Lancastria's level of 1975.

In May 1983 Greater Lancastria merged with the North Midland to form United Co-operatives. During the 1980s a number of other co-ops came under United's wing. Thus, by 1987, United represented a continuous trading corridor from the Lakes to the Midlands, but only two of the half-dozen societies which it had taken over were profitable. Indeed, it was only after major management restructuring and re-investment that it was able to make a surplus of £7 million in 1989. United's last balance sheet before its merger in 1991 into United Norwest, however, revealed that it had record profits of £11.3 million on sales of £345 million and that its commercial outlets comprised one hundred 'Lateshop' convenience stores, sixty-nine supermarkets and eighteen 'Normid' superstores and hypermarkets.

When it was established in 1982 the Norwest Pioneers was the sixth largest independent co-op with an estimated turnover of more than £140 million

All three buildings shown here were part of the CWS headquarters. The central building, No. 1 Balloon Street, is still standing, while the one on the right, built in 1911, was demolished in the 1970s and is now the site of the Co-operative Bank headquarters *(Co-operative Union).*

derived from seven superstores, one hundred other supermarkets, plus department stores and extensive dairy and other service operations. 'Pioneers' was regrettably dropped from its name in 1985–6, because it was adopted by a new honorary society. By 1991 on the eve of its amalgamation it had a total of 259 retailing outlets and a trading surplus of £6.9 million on sales of £214 million.

United Norwest was created on 20 April 1991 after the members of the United and Norwest Societies overwhelmingly voted in favour of amalgamation. The new society had an estimated combined turnover of £560 million or 8.5 per cent of the total co-op trade in the United Kingdom. It employed 10,000 staff in 400 trading units, including 29 superstores, 8 department stores, 115 convenience stores, 100 supermarkets and food branches, 39 travel bureaux, 27 pharmacies and retail garages, filling stations and several funeral homes and it served a huge area, extending from the Lake District in the north to Staffordshire in the south and Greater Manchester in the east to parts of Merseyside in the west. In fact, it represents one of the largest retail co-ops in Europe and the largest independent society in the United Kingdom.

Co-operative Retail Services Ltd is the name adopted by the CWS Retail Society, which had been formed in 1934 to promote trade in 'co-op deserts' and help struggling societies. Between 1936 and 1991 CRS accepted 177 independent societies, mainly concentrated in Wales, the south-west and Yorkshire, into its ranks. The CRS in Lancashire, however, is largely confined to small pockets in the north-east of the county and around Merseyside. The Burnley and Padiham societies, which amalgamated in 1968 to become the Pendle Co-operative Society, merged with the CRS in 1971, and the former Leigh and Liverpool Co-ops were also taken over. Originally, independent societies became branches of the CRS, but in the 1970s these branches were grouped into regions and in 1985 six large sectors replaced the existing twelve regions and the trading departments came more directly under the control of the National Management team in Manchester. Both the CWS and the CRS retain close business links, but attempts to merge them into one large society have proved unsuccessful so far.

In terms of organisation, all the CRS stores in Lancashire conform to the national CRS pattern with increasing specialisation and marketing labels. In the Food Division, for example, there is a three-tier structure of shopping outlets: 'Leo's' or the larger supermarkets, the 'market fresh' for medium-sized stores, and the small, local community 'stop and shop' stores. In 1992 national membership of the CRS stood at 1,436,000, there were 10,765 full-time and a further 12,802 part-time employees and the turnover totalled

The Pioneer Service Station, one of the many departments and services run by the Rochdale Society in the 1960s *(The Rochdale Equitable Pioneers' Society: an illustrated souvenir [Co-operative Union, 1967], p. 27).*

£1,496,605,000. Turnover in the Lancashire Region (in the north-east) for the year ending January 1993 stood at £50,291,845 and that of the Liverpool Region £30,614,425. In 1988 the CRS launched its Shareholder Card, the modern equivalent to dividend payments, with a 5 per cent discount given on all purchases at participating food and dry goods stores. In order to combat the competition of European food discounters the CRS has recently converted many of its Leo's stores, like those at Park Road and Breck Road in Liverpool, to the 'Pioneer' concept. In the Non-Food Division, department stores, including Pendle House in the town centre at Burnley, are managed under the 'Living' concept, whereas 'Homeworld' is the name given to the large out-of-town outlets. The stores in the CRS Northern Sector have undergone a rolling programme of improvements and remerchandising. The summer of 1982 witnessed the refurbishment of the Quality House Department Store in Burnley and the opening of a 46,000 sq.ft. Leo's superstore costing £3,500,000

Krazy Kuts, a large supermarket, was established in a disused bakery premises in the Rochdale area. It operated on a very low profit margin, cash only, no deliveries or services, yet selling nationally advertised and branded goods at cut prices. This was another example of the continuing pioneering spirit of the movement *(The Rochdale Equitable Pioneers' Society: an illustrated souvenir [Co-operative Union, 1967], p. 27).*

in Curzon Street, Burnley, a flagship for the CRS in the north. More recently other stores have been refurbished.

The Co-op, therefore, is very much a big business organisation and has had some recent commercial successes. Its initiatives seem at odds with the image of bureaucratic inefficiency and falling profit margins often associated with it since the Second World War. The latest *Co-operative Statistics* for the year 1992 show that the movement's total turnover amounted to £7.3 billion divided between the Food Division, with £5.1 billion, and the Non-Food Division, with £2.2 billion. The fluctuating fortunes of the movement, however, have often resulted in its receiving a bad press, being described as antiquated, shabby and lower class, a 'retail dinosaur' and even a 'sleeping giant'.

The Co-op and the Community

As we have seen, the Co-op was always intended to be much more than a retail business and throughout its existence it has sought to put into practice the principles of early promoters, producing a commitment to welfare, education and community provision which is unparalleled by any other business organisation. Societies' jubilee publications which appeared earlier in the century always stressed not just their business success but the wider ambitions of the movement which had underpinned the Rochdale Pioneers' principles. The Pendleton Co-operative pamphlet of 1910, for example, argued that

> Co-operation is not merely buying goods at a Store and watching and waiting with more or less patience for a dividend; it is not investing money with a view to drawing the best possible interest with the least risk; it is not even assisting to establish additional premises to undertake new business; but applying the principles to every phase and condition of life, and making it the driving force of a whole existence.

Consequently, local co-operative societies frequently played an important part in the wider community, providing education, social organisations and facilities, entertainments, donations to charities and investment in local business and housing. Although the rationalisation of co-op business and the continued amalgamation of societies into increasingly large units, together with growing State provision and changing social habits, have clearly affected the nature of active member participation and community involvement, many co-operators have sought to ensure that democratic and social ideals have not been sacrificed in the quest for business efficiency. Although the social role of the Co-op has contracted ever since the inter-war period, and especially in the post-war years as both total membership and active involvement fell, the movement's commitment to the local community has not disappeared: rather it has been forced to re-think its educational policies and social activities.

Education and Social Welfare

The Co-operative movement's commitment to providing education was particularly important at a time when there were few alternative educational facilities for working-class people. For the most part co-operative educational provision consisted of the provision of libraries, newsrooms and publications, but it also included formal classes, for both members and staff. Classes and lectures were partly designed to provide a general education for members, teaching them about the history and principles of the Co-operative movement, so that they could become better citizens and knowledgeable customers able to take an active role in the running of their own societies. Towards the end of the nineteenth century, technical classes for employees to train them in retail management were also developed.

This commitment to education was particularly evident in the early societies in Lancashire, with the Rochdale Pioneers running fourteen libraries with fourteen thousand volumes by 1877. Provision increased in the late nineteenth century. In 1884, for example, the movement as a whole expended £18,000 each year on education, over £11,000 of this in Lancashire, but only 37 per cent of societies set aside funds for the purpose. A national survey in 1895, however, revealed that approximately 60 per cent of the societies undertook some type of educational activities – though few laid aside the full 2.5 per cent of profits suggested by the Co-operative Union. Educational provision, however, varied from society to society, depending on size, wealth and principles. Bolton society's annual expenditure on education was the highest in the county at £3,632, or 2 per cent of profits in 1914 and the results of its investments could still be seen into the inter-war period. In 1932 it had a library of sixteen thousand volumes, took twenty-one daily newspapers, sixty-seven weekly newspapers and thirty-five monthly magazines. On the other hand, other large societies, like Pendleton, appear to have had little interest in the educational objectives of the movement. Smaller societies in the north of the county, like Dalton-in-Furness, also spent a proportion of its income on education resulting, by 1893, in the provision of four reading rooms, the purchase of one hundred daily and weekly newspapers and a library of three thousand volumes with a weekly issue of six hundred, but this contrasted with the situation in the neighbouring and much larger Barrow-in-Furness society which, throughout the whole period from 1885 to 1910, had no educational fund.

These initiatives continued up to the Second World War and were promoted by societies' Education Committees and the Co-operative Educational Committees' Associations. The Co-operative College was founded in 1919, and youth organisations formed to promote co-op values and principles. Local education activities remained important throughout the period but, with

LIST OF NEWSPAPERS, PERIODICALS, ETC.,

Supplied to the Central News-room.

DAILY:
Birmingham Morning News
Bradford Observer
Daily News, 3 copies
Daily Telegraph, 2 copies
Leeds Mercury, 2 copies
Liverpool Daily Post
Liverpool Mercury, 2 copies
Lloyd's List
London Times, 2 copies
Manchester Courier
Manchester Evening Mail
Manchester Evening News
Manchester Examiner, 2 copies
" " Evening Edition
Manchester Guardian, 3 copies
Newcastle Daily Chronicle
Pall Mall Gazette
Scotsman
Standard
Yorkshire Post

BI-WEEKLY:
London Gazette
Preston Guardian and Supplement

WEEKLY:
Alliance News
Athenæum
Beehive
Ben Brierley's Journal
Bow Bells
Bury Times
Carlisle Journal
Christian World
Co-operative News, 2 copies
Cottage Gardener, Journal of Horticulture
Economist
Engineer
English Mechanic
Family Herald
Field
Free Lance
Freeman, A Baptist Record
Freeman's Journal
Fun
Furniture Gazette
Graphic, 2 copies
Halifax Courier
Harper's Weekly
Illustrated London News
Inquirer
Judy
Labourers' Union Chronicle
Lamp
Lancaster Guardian
Leeds Times
Liverpool Weekly Albion
London Examiner
London Journal
London Reader
London Spectator
Manchester Weekly Courier
Manchester Weekly Times & Supplement

WEEKLY *(continued)*:
Mark Lane Express
Methodist Recorder
Money Market Review
National Reformer
Nonconformist
Oldham Chronicle
Phonetic Journal
Punch
Quiver
Reynold's Newspaper
Rochdale Observer, 2 copies
Rochdale Times, 2 copies
Saturday Review
Sunday at Home
World

MONTHLY:
Agricultural Economist
All the Year Round
Arbitrator
Art Journal
Belgravia
Blackwood's Magazine
Bookseller
Bradshaw's Guide
British Workman
Cassell's Magazine
Chambers's Journal
Congregationalist
Contemporary Review
Cornhill Magazine
Dietetic Reformer
Financial Reformer
Fortnightly Review
Fraser's Magazine
Gentleman's Magazine
Good Words
Herald of Peace
Homœopathic World
Investor's Monthly Manual
Leisure Hour
Liberator
London Society
Macmillan's Magazine
Notes and Queries
Once a Week
Practical Magazine
Scribner's Monthly
St. James' Magazine
Temple Bar
XL Railway Guide

QUARTERLY:
British Postal Guide
British Quarterly Review
Edinburgh Review
Mind, The
New Quarterly Magazine
Popular Science Review
Quarterly Review
Spencer's Principles of Psychology
Westminster Review

Examples of the range of material available to members (above and opposite) in the catalogue of the library of the Rochdale Equitable Pioneers' Society, 1876.

NOTICE.

The Members of the Society are informed that there is kept in the Library and News-room, Toad Lane, the undermentioned

SCIENTIFIC INSTRUMENTS,

Which can be used in the room by Members, free of charge, or hired out at the undermentioned charges, on application to the Librarian.

TELESCOPES.—One large and powerful Telescope, with terrestrial and astronomical eye pieces, fitted with all necessary appliances for day and night observations. Terms :—For one day, 4d.; three days, 8d.; and for one week, 1s. Two Tourists' or Field Telescopes, fitted with leather cases and slings. Terms :—Each, 2d. per day, or 9d. per week.

MICROSCOPE.—A new Compound Achromatic Microscope, with ¼in., 1in., and 2in. object glasses, and two eye pieces : there are also along with it about 170 glass slides on which are mounted objects in Natural History, Mineralogy, Photography, &c. Terms :—Instrument with box, containing 4 dozen objects, 2d. per day; and 1d. per day for each additional box of 4 dozen objects.

STEREOSCOPES.—Two Box Stereoscopes, each containing 100 miscellaneous views, 2d. per day. Two Box Stereoscopes, each containing 50 miscellaneous views, 1d. per day. Three Hand Stereoscopes, 1d. per day, with case of 50 views, and 1d. per day for every additional case of 50 views.

MAGNETIC BATTERIES.—One large battery, 3d. per day; two smaller batteries, 2d. each per day.

MARINE, TOURIST, OPERA, AND FIELD GLASSES, 1d. per day.

ZOETROPE.—Zoetrope, or Wheel of Life, with 3 dozen slides, 2d. per day.

COSMOSCOPE.—The Committee wish to call special attention to a new and miscellaneous collection of 250 large Photo. Views, 8¼in. by 6¼in., of English and Foreign Scenery, Statuary, &c., &c., taken by Frith. The Cosmoscope is a newly-invented handsome instrument for giving magnified perspective, and beautiful stereoscopic effect to the above views. Terms :—Cosmoscope, with a portfolio containing 50 views, 6d. per day; and 3d. for each additional portfolio of 50 views.

Members are particularly requested to use the Cosmoscope, Views, and all the other Instruments with the greatest care; and in all cases persons using any of the above-named articles will be held responsible for their being returned uninjured.

falling profit margins, co-ops found it increasingly difficult to finance them by the inter-war period, while the growth of municipal educational services and libraries undermined the need for some of them. The outbreak of war spelled the end of many of the Co-op's educational and social welfare activites; for example the number of students enrolled in classes declined sharply.

Since the war, however, there have been initiatives to enhance and preserve the Co-op's role. Education Committees and the Co-operative Educational Committees' Associations have been replaced by the Member Relations Committees and the National Co-op Education Association and, in line with national trends, Member Relations Officers and Committees in Lancashire no longer provide formal educational classes for member and employees; instead, this function has been taken over by the Co-operative College. In 1945 the College and Education Department moved to Stanford Hall, a former stately home near Loughborough. It offers courses for new members and directors, as well as the Capability Certificate in Co-operative Studies and is currently developing national archives of co-operative film and oral history.

A major development in co-op education since the Second World War has been the growing links forged with schools and colleges. The Warrington Region of the United Norwest Society, for example, liaises with nine schools and has strong ties with the Loushers Lane Special School. The Co-operative movement can not only be studied as a topic under such disciplines as business management and local history, but also co-operative values and methods of learning can be used in the classroom. Moreover, the Co-op has been keen to promote vocational training under such initiatives as the Schools Curriculum Industry Partnership. Consequently, the movement has made considerable resources available to schools and organised placements and training days for teachers. Recently the United Norwest Society took two Stockport teachers on secondment and funded them to design an educational pack for key stages one and two of the National Curriculum. As part of a national scheme to encourage youngsters to establish and run their own co-op enterprises within school a second Teen Co-ops Project was launched in 1992 covering thirty schools throughout the north-west and involving both the United Norwest Society and the CRS Lancashire and Merseyside Regions in collaboration with the Lancashire Co-op Development Agency. More specifically, the CRS has developed a number of computer software packages for use in schools and colleges, including 'Odd Job', a worker co-operative simulation activity. It has also compiled a

Special needs children from Nelson, Burnley and Colne enjoying a 'Bit of a Do' *(Liz Chadwick, CRS Burnley).*

database of those educationalists interested in co-operative learning. In recent years the Member Relations Department in the CRS Lancashire Region has supported a number of school-based schemes, including a Fun Day called 'A Bit of a Do' for special needs children from Nelson, Burnley and Colne; and a Natural Garden Project at Leo's superstore in Burnley, again involving youngsters with special needs.

Apart from schools work, societies in Lancashire continue to support the Co-op's own auxiliary youth organisations, like the Woodcraft Folk which was promoted as an alternative to the scouting movement. In 1993 there was a total of 680 groups throughout the United Kingdom, including 163 in the north of England. The Folk's buzzword in recent years has been 'regionalisation', as it has introduced regional conferences to strengthen its structure and identity. At the last count twenty-six Woodcraft folk branches were to be found in United Norwest's trading area. To help raise public awareness the first ever

Woodcraft Week was organised in 1992 and the Levenshulme group in Manchester held an open day at Alma Park School as part of the 1993 Woodcraft Week. Similarly, the CRS support the Woodcraft Folk, not only financially but also in kind, providing meeting places, publicity literature and training for local leaders. By January 1990 the CRS was backing 251 Woodcraft groups nationwide with branches at Burnley, Padiham, Leigh and Colne as well as groups in the CRS Merseyside Region.

Co-operative societies in Lancashire were also involved in other aspects of community provision, including investing surplus capital in the shares of local companies and in property. This was not confined to commercial and industrial property; it also included domestic housing. By 1906 co-operative societies nationally had invested almost £10 million in housing; over £6.5 million on mortgages for members to build or buy houses, over £1 million on houses which had been sold to members, and over £2 million on houses for rent. In 1868, for example, the Bolton society set up a special department to provide a mortgage service to help members to buy their own homes and by 1959 21,000 members had borrowed in excess of £5 million. Similarly, the Farnworth & Kearsley Society (1873) ran its own mortgage scheme with over 12,000 houses being purchased by members by 1923. Wigan began its housing purchasing scheme in 1896, whilst Chorley opened its mortgage department in 1908. In Lonsdale North of the Sands, four societies built houses, although only one of these, Dalton-in-Furness, operated a house-purchasing scheme. In 1903 Dalton's representative at a district conference claimed that two-thirds of its members were home owners, largely due to the efforts of the society. Council house building and the expansion of mortgage facilities, however, contributed to the decline of these activities in the twentieth century.

Before the Welfare State the movement also acted as a self-help organisation with local co-op societies organising social services and supporting charitable ventures and good causes in the community. The movement also cared for the health of its members at convalescent homes managed by the CWS, each affiliated society paying towards their upkeep and in return being allowed to nominate their members for treatment. There were two such homes in the north-west, one at Gilsland on the Cumberland/Northumberland border, opened in 1902, and another at Blackpool, opened in 1906.

The Women's Co-operative Guild, founded in 1883, was particularly important in pioneering a number of important social campaigns. This auxiliary body of the Co-op was the oldest and largest democratic and

Gilsland is a source of spa water and had long been a place to visit for cures before the present building (now called the Gilsland Spa Hotel) was opened to the public in 1886. The estate was bought by the co-operative society for £21,000 in 1901 and was run as a convalescent home. During the First World War soldiers came to recuperate before returning to the front line and during the Second it was used as a maternity home for women from bomb target areas, especially Tyneside and Teesside. It is now owned by the North-Eastern Co-op and operates as a hotel *(Anne Addiman Photographic Collection)*.

voluntary association of working-class women. The Guild had four main strands of policy: the propagation of Co-operation; citizenship campaigns; women's and children's rights and welfare; and local community work, including charities. Its members were important in politicising and publicising domestic issues and providing an outlet at a time when there were few social/educational opportunities for respectable working-class women. However, the Guild's relationship with the Co-operative movement was not always smooth; indeed, their radical policies, for example their divorce reform

The work of the Women's Guilds has always been an important aspect of the co-operative movement. Seen here with their respective banners are (above) the Lancaster branch at the turn of the century and (opposite) the Rochdale Pioneers branch celebrating its centenary
(Lancaster City Museum and Co-operative Union).

campaign, led to their grant being suspended by the Co-operative Union between 1914 and 1918.

Six branches of the Guild were formed in 1883, but only one of these was in Lancashire, at Rochdale. Indeed, in the early years there was much more interest in the Guild in the southern societies. By 1889 of fifty-one branches only seven were situated in Lancashire and Yorkshire. By 1921 there were over one thousand branches, and by 1939 87,246 members, but growth was still not reflected in the north, where membership remained relatively stagnant through the inter-war years. However, despite the Guild's southern bias,

Lancashire did play a part in its development. Several notable leaders of the Guild were based in and around Lancashire, notably Margaret Llewellyn Davies who was General Secretary from 1889 to 1921. She was based in Kirkby Lonsdale, just outside the northern border of the county. Additionally, the Bolton Guild, under the leadership of Sarah Reddish, was notable for its activities, including the Bolton School for Mothers founded in 1910–11. Many societies in the county supported Women's Guild branches from the late nineteenth century to beyond the Second World War.

Co-operative societies were also major benefactors of local charities, those in Lancashire donating £2,356 to local charities in 1889 and £16,393 by 1914. Many societies also granted free use of their premises for charity fund-raising events and contributed to disaster funds, such as the Fleetwood flood victims of 1927. Another facet of the Co-op's charity work was the distribution of food aid and the opening of recreation facilities for the local unemployed and destitute. In 1921, for example, the Farnworth & Kearsley Society complied with the local Education Committee's request to supply free school meals. It also supported the Farnworth Unemployment and Right to Work Fund of that year, the Welfare Voluntary Fund in 1924 and the Local Distress Fund during the miners' strike of 1926, although the question of whether co-ops should pay dividends on the food vouchers presented by recipients of outdoor relief became a point of contention. Societies also provided assistance to weavers in the strikes of the early 1930s.

Much of this has been preserved into the post-war years, although the form and extent of it have changed to meet the new conditions. Lancashire Member Relations liaise with auxiliary bodies like the Women's Guilds and Woodcraft Folk, and continue to undertake valuable charity work. Because of the deep-seated traditions of co-operation in the county, a wider range of local community groups seems to be in evidence than in other parts of the country, and in many respects there is a remarkable degree of continuity in the nature of member participation and local community involvement in Lancashire. In particular, co-operators in the Lancashire Region of the CRS continue to maintain strong links with the Labour Party and trade union movement and are showing renewed interest in other forms of collective enterprise, such as credit unions and housing and producer co-ops.

The movement has continued to pursue an active role in local community affairs and still encourages members and employees to participate in public life. Co-operators are encouraged to become school governors and training courses are organised by the Co-op College. More importantly, as part of its major reforms in 1985 the CRS adopted a Statement of Social Objectives, which embrace the consumer, the membership, the employees and the wider society. One of these aims is to 'meet within the limitations of the resources available, social and community needs which cannot be met sufficiently by other agencies and do not fall within the responsibility of the state'. Through this the spirit of the Co-operative Commonwealth is retained, as it compasses wider concerns such as health and safety and environmental issues, with support for international peace and understanding, including trade with developing nations. In 1988 the CRS published the first of its biannual Social Reports and two years later the new post of Social Policy Officer was created. It has also compiled a register of new and active members, which allows it to maintain greater contact, as it regularly sends out information.

The Education Department of the Co-operative Union also runs a special Community Award scheme, whereby the local sub-committees of individual societies can nominate local charities and community groups for small financial grants. In 1993 the United Norwest Society made presentations to Mission Vision, a Wigan-based group dealing with drug and alcohol abuse, and to the Pemberton Physically Handicapped and Able Bodied Club. In the same year the Merseyside winner of the Co-op Union's Media Award was again *Silk Road News*, a local newspaper for the Chinese community in Liverpool. Furthermore, in line with the CRS's policy of promoting better world-wide relations, a multi-cultural art festival was organised in Burnley's Asian community, and International Women's Day was celebrated in Leigh.

With the amalgamation of many societies and the rationalisation of trade during the last fifty years, most retail co-ops do not undertake their own productive ventures or invest in local businesses to use up excess capital. However, the CRS remains committed to 'extend the co-operative sector of the economy as a form of social ownership and encourage understanding of co-operative forms of organisation'. The mainstream Co-operative movement often works in conjunction with the government-sponsored Co-operative Development Agency and local authorities to achieve these ends and help local people launch their own co-operative ventures. With pockets of urban decay, high unemployment and low-wage economies, Lancashire has been especially receptive to different types of co-operation, such as credit unions, housing and worker co-ops and LETS (Local Exchange Trade System). At present there are three credit unions in Burnley, seventy-eight housing co-ops on Merseyside, and in terms of worker co-ops successful enterprises in north-east Lancashire include the 'Just Dust' community co-op in Colne, which is an outlet for third-world goods, the New Era, a community business, and the Altham Hardwood Centre.

The movement continues to provide a social service and there is a conscious attempt in Lancashire to centre activities at the stores and thus highlight the links between trade and social ideals. For instance, the CRS produces customer information leaflets and brief histories of some of its former societies, and all its major food stores now contain information stands giving details of

Member Relations activities and health education. The Leo's Superstore at Leigh has taken part in the CRS's 'healthy living' campaigns, and both the Leigh and Burnley Leo's have arranged late-night shopping evenings for the elderly and disabled prior to Christmas. Most notably, the Co-op maintains less profitable stores in poorer areas for the elderly, immobile and socially disadvantaged in what it describes as 'the social dividend'. One such store is the United Norwest's Late Shop in the West End of Morecambe. Trading departments also run specialist services caring for local people with the Health Care Division of the United Norwest recently attracting a £10,000 grant from the Department of Health to help operate its screening programme for blood pressure and heart risk factors for both staff and customers. The Division also tests for eye defects and has two non-smoking clinics, besides which its pharmacists visit nursing homes and provide a delivery service for the house-bound. CRS milkmen are encouraged to keep an eye on sick and old customers and to inform social services of potential problems. This is one example of a long-established link with local authorities.

Many co-op employees also freely help with charity fund-raising. Donations range from small initiatives by individuals, small stores and trading departments in some larger stores to aid local charities, to large sales promotions and annual fund-raising campaigns, including national appeals, and support for one-off emergency disaster funds. Recent local efforts by staff in Lancashire have included the Rochdale Shoe Department, the St Helens area and the Capesthorne Late Shop in Warrington, which respectively raised £259 for the RSPCA in 1991, £200 for the Alder Hey Children's Hospital in 1992, and £226 for the victims of the Warrington IRA bomb attack in the summer of 1993. Two large-scale sales promotions by the United Norwest in 1993 were a voucher scheme in conjunction with BBC's *Blue Peter* presenter Anthea Turner to provide games and sports equipment for schools and nurseries, and a banana sales promotion which raised £11,000 for the British Heart Foundation and Cancer Research. Co-op employees also contribute to annual charity appeals like the BBC's *Children in Need*, and United Norwest runs its own annual charity fund-raising event which since 1989 has donated at least £12,000 each year to various organisations, supporting a children's hospice and treatment for breast cancer, diabetes and multiple sclerosis. Among other charitable grants the CRS gave £1,000 to Enterprise North West in 1988–9 and £5,000 to the Hillsborough Football Disaster Fund, while the United Norwest Society made a donation to the Greater Manchester Police relief convoy to Bosnia. Besides financial support, United Norwest organises competitions and entertainments for the disabled. For the last fifteen years its Northern Region has staged an annual two-day craft exhibition featuring the work of the physically handicapped. In 1993 it was held at Runshaw College in Leyland and attracted entries from thirteen towns, with prizes awarded to social service centres in Blackburn and Lancaster. Another notable event for the disabled is the Jubilee Games, which takes place each year in Bolton.

Community Activities

As this implies, the Co-op was, and is, even more than a socially concerned trading organisation; it has also been interested in promoting entertainment and recreation. Local societies frequently provided entertainments for

Preston Industrial Co-operative Society Limited issued 7,000 copies of the *Preston Co-operative Record* each month. This contained official notices of the society, details of charitable work, information on excursions, field days, concerts, entertainments, etc. This particular field day was on 9 August 1902, Coronation Day. As many as 15,000 children attended such days *(Memento of the Guild Merchant 1902 [CWS, 1902], p. 60).*

CHORLEY CO-OPERATIVE SOCIETY, LIMITED.

TERMS FOR HIRE

OF THE

Co-operative Hall.

AND CONDITIONS FOR LETTING THE SAME.

PRIVATE BALL	1	1	0
LECTURES, ENTERTAINMENTS, CONCERTS, CLUB OR TRADE MEETINGS	0	10	0
MEAT TEAS (not less than 80 Persons)	1/3 per head.		
,, (less than 80 Persons)	1/6 ,,		
PLAIN TEAS (not less than 80 Persons)	9d. ,,		
,, (less than 80 Persons	1/- ,,		

Parties taking the Hall to find their own Tea Spoons, Knives and Forks, Tea Urns, and Waiters, for which a reasonable sum will be allowed.

All Tea Parties will have the use of Piano free.

The Committee to have the privilege of entering the Hall during any Lecture, Entertainment, or other engagement of the Hall.

If the Hall be used for a different purpose than that for which it was taken, the Manager, Secretary, or any of the Committee of the Society, may at any time put a stop to the proceedings.

Smoking is strictly prohibited, and the Lessee shall expel any persons found Smoking or otherwise misbehaving themselves in the Hall.

A Deposit of 5/- will be required before the Hall will be considered by us to be engaged to any applicant, and, further, any person taking the Hall will be held liable for the whole amount due (less deposit paid) for the length of time he has engaged the Hall, whether he fulfils his engagement or not.

Parties occupying the Hall will be held responsible for any damage sustained during their term of occupation.

The Caretaker will prepare and heat the Hall, open and close the doors, and attend to the gas.

Parties occupying the Hall after 11 o'clock p.m. will be charged at the rate of 5/- per hour or fractional part of an hour extra, except in cases specially agreed upon.

No article will be allowed to be sold in the Hall without the consent of the Committee of Management.

The cost of hiring rooms was normally competitive. Some of the conditions seem amusing nowadays *(Lancashire County Library, Chorley Local Studies Collection)*.

members, employees and local people. By the end of the nineteenth century, a number of the larger societies in the county, like Bolton, Oldham, Chorley and Manchester & Salford, also produced their own 'in-house' publications for members to promote their activities and to encourage loyalty and create a sense of belonging amongst members. These were also used to promote wider co-operative ideals. From the 1920s most ceased producing such magazines, preferring to place news of their own society in the pages provided in the movement's national newspapers, *The Wheatsheaf* and *The Co-operative News*. Only the Manchester & Salford Society continued to produce its own magazine until the late 1950s.

A lasting and visible sign of co-operative involvement in the local community were the recreation halls. The largest societies had a number of such halls, each seating several hundred people. The Bolton society had two, with the capacity to hold 350 and 500, whilst in St Helens the society had three halls accommodating 750, 500 and 250 people. At Carnforth the single Co-operative Hall was the main focus of town social life up to the Second World War. This, of course, was not the case with the smallest village societies, although some used rooms above their shop premises for social or educational gatherings. Co-op halls and rooms, sometimes including catering facilities, were not just used by the societies themselves, but were made available to other working-class organisations to hold meetings and social events. The committee of Farnworth & Kearsley, for instance, granted the hire of their hall on favourable terms to the Transport Workers' Union every first Sunday in the month in the early 1920s. In many towns during the inter-war period premises represented an alternative working-class power base to the local middle-class establishment. Many co-operators were also town councillors and retail societies often competed for local authority contracts, including the provision of school milk and hospital services. The CWS and the retail societies of Manchester participated in the city's annual civic celebrations, although co-operative involvement in local affairs was not always welcomed.

Social activities included dances, whist drives, choirs, competitions, children's parties and concerts. For instance, the larger societies, including Bolton and St Helens, established their own music and drama groups which gave regular performances, and during the 1920s and 1930s large co-ops, like Manchester & Salford, even acquired their own recreational centres. As well as cultural activities co-ops also organised sports, as teams of employees competed in the CWS football and cricket leagues in the 1930s. An important

The Assembly Rooms in Holyoake House, Manchester, seen here after the refurbishment of the 1930s. The hall could seat 350 people. The portraits are (left to right): Edward Vansittart Neale (1810–1892), first general secretary of the Co-operative Union; George Jacob Holyoake (1817–1906) in whose honour the building was named in 1911; Jesse Clement Gray (1854–1912), second general secretary of the Union. *(Co-operative Union.)*

feature in the social calendar of many societies was the annual carnival, gala or festival held to celebrate their success and to recruit new members. Such occasions would consist of floats, sports and a children's gala with food, in the form of tea, generally provided, and often served, by the Women's Guild.

Equally popular were the day trips run by many societies. *Bolton Co-operative Record* was full of advertisements for such excursions. A large number of Lancashire co-ops, both big and small, also had holiday clubs – including Accrington & Church, Shawforth and Withnell Industrial Co-operative Societies. These helped working-class people save up for their week away through penny bank schemes and the accumulation of their dividends. *The Producer* reported how Lancashire folk used the dividend they obtained from the stores to save for the annual Wakes Weeks. The sums involved could be extremely large; for the Oldham Wakes Week, starting on the fourth Saturday in August 1919, £200,000 was paid out in holiday money to the workers. The following amusing account by the late film critic, Leslie Halliwell, is of a holiday arranged by the Education Committee of the Bolton Society:

> the events of the year were the 'trips', cheap holiday packages offered in Wakes Week at the end of June, with committee men acting as couriers . . . We were due to go to Lugano – it would have been Dad's turn in 1940 – but the War stopped us. In the previous summer, though, the whole family (at reduced rates) helped him shepherd 400 people to, from and around the Isle of Man. Everybody agreed that he did a grand job, handing out rosettes, chatting up the bandleader, and forever checking numbers.

The cost of holiday saving schemes ranged from 3*d.* to 10*s.* per week. A campaign was even orchestrated during the inter-war years to allow co-op holidaymakers to shop at other seaside societies, like Blackpool, and still collect their dividends. With a membership of 45,712 and a sales turnover of £1,687,726, Blackpool was one of the ten largest societies in the North Western Section by 1939.

Arguably, the high points of any society's existence were the celebrations of its various anniversaries. These events were extremely large affairs and in addition to the entertainments, members were given commemorative items, mainly cups, plates, teapots or boxes. The Eccles Society Jubilee, held in 1907, cost in excess of £2,250 and included trade displays, tableaux, a procession, dancing, refreshments and entertainments. A souvenir box was given to all members, those over sixty years of age were invited to a free tea with entertainment and the employees were offered a free dinner and tea. Children's fêtes were also held. Where societies had branch stores in surrounding villages, the members from these areas were generally brought in to share in the celebrations. The celebrations to honour the centenary of the Rochdale Pioneers in 1944 took on an international form, which were unfortunately curtailed by the war, but they included a special 'Pageant of the People', a play performed at Wembley Stadium and throughout the country.

These community activities were particularly prominent in Lancashire and remained important in the close-knit, working-class communities which had

WHITSUNTIDE EXCURSIONS.

Whit-Thursday, June 7th, 1900.

BLACKPOOL. Leaving Trinity Street Station at 6-35, 7-55, 9-20, 10-18 a.m., 1-57, 2-45, 6-15, 6-40, 7-15, 7-30 p.m.
5 DAYS. **Fare 4/- each.**

SOUTHPORT. Leaving Trinity Street Station at 6-55 and 9-5 a.m., 5-45 and 6-45 p.m.
4 DAYS. **Fare 3/3 each.**

MORECAMBE. **(Via Hellifield).** Leaving Trinity Street Station at 6-55 and 9-58 a.m., 2-38 and 6-3 p.m.
5 DAYS. **Fare 4/6 each.**

LLANDUDNO. Leaving Great Moor Street Station L. & N. W.) at 7-55 and 9-10 a.m., 12-15, 3-20, 4-15 and 6-15 p.m.
5 DAYS. **Fare 7/- each.**

SCOTLAND.
GREENOCK, AND **GLASGOW.** **For 4 or 8 days.** Train leaves Trinity Street Station at 11-10 p.m.; returning from St. Enoch Station, Glasgow, at 3 p.m. on June 11th, **9/6;** or Friday, June 15th, **16/-.** This train calls at Farnworth at 11-0 p.m., and Moses Gate at 11-5 p.m.

CARLISLE, EDINBURGH, AND **GLASGOW.** **By the Waverley Route.** The train will leave Trinity Street Station at 11-20 p.m.; Farnworth at 11-10 p.m.; Moses Gate at 11-15 p.m. Returning from Glasgow at 1-0 p.m.; Edinburgh (Waverley Station), 2-25 p.m.; and Carlisle, 5-45 p.m., Monday, June 11th, or on Friday, June 15th.

FARES { **CARLISLE - - - 4 Days, 7/6; 8 Days, 9/9.**
EDINBURGH or GLASGOW - „ 9/6; „ 16/-.

LONDON. **(St. Pancras Station). For 3 or 6 Days.** Via the Peak of Derbyshire. Leaving Trinity Street Station at 10-55 p.m., calling at Moses Gate at 10-59 p.m., Farnworth, 11-2 p.m., and Stoneclough, 11-5 p.m.; returning on June 10th from St. Pancras Station, London, at 11-30 p.m.; and on June 13th from St. Pancras Station at 12-0 p.m.

Fares for 3 Days, 12/6; for 6 Days, 16/-.

ISLE OF MAN. By the Quickest Route, via Fleetwood. Leaving Trinity Street Station at 11-35 and 11-45 p.m., Third Class and Steerage.

Fares { To return on Monday, June 11th or Tuesday, June 12th - **9/-**
To return up to and including June 15th (via Fleetwood) - **9/9**

CHILDREN UNDER TWELVE YEARS OF AGE HALF-FARES.

Tickets may be obtained at any of the Society's Stores.

The co-op has a history of involvement in the holiday industry.
The advertisement (opposite) from the *Bolton Co-operative Record* of June 1900 shows the range of holidays on offer then. *(Jean Turnbull.)*
The photograph above shows the travel shop which opened in Preston in 1995.
(Anne Addiman Photographic Collection.)

spawned co-operation through the economic depression and the stagnation of the cotton and coal industries, despite the rise of alternative commercial entertainments such as the cinema. Lancashire Member Relations have made conscious attempts to preserve this social role in the post-war period, the way things are run very much reflecting the structures and practices of former co-op societies before they were amalgamated. During the late 1970s and early 1980s, for example, the Norwest Society had a policy to maintain as many members' groups as possible and United Norwest still supports the old auxiliary bodies, although it sees the future in single interest groups like the sports clubs and brass bands, some of which receive four-figure sums in funding. The old Norwest Society was particularly good at linking Member Relations to the trading departments because of its strong tradition of helping local charities, whereas the old United areas had a tradition of sponsoring

The 'Jubilee Teapot' produced to commemorate the Kirkby-in-Furness Co-operative Society Jubilee 1862–1912. *(Jean Turnbull.)*

more community events, including the Southport swimming gala. On the other hand, the Lancashire and Liverpool Regions of the CRS represent part of a national framework, thus many of their Member Relations activities are part of central directives, although there are additional informal groups in Burnley and Leigh.

It has not all been plain sailing, with the relative success of the Woodcraft folk, for example, not being matched by the Co-operative Women's Guild, which has experienced a decline in membership since the Second World War, largely due to a failure to attract younger recruits. Nationally, the year 1939 was the high point in the Guild's fortunes; thereafter it witnessed a steady decline in membership, dropping to just over 35,000 in 1965 and to approximately 5,000 in 1991. In Lancashire, there were 283 branches in 1945 with a total membership of just over 12,000; by 1992 the comparative figures were 20 and 340 respectively. However, the county continues to play its part in the

The Woodcraft Folk celebrated their sixtieth anniversary in 1985. Here a group of young people returns from a holiday abroad.
(Co-operative Union.)

national movement with Northern Region branches at Marton and Bispham and Central Region branches at Ashton-in-Makerfield, Bolton, Earlstown and Higher Irlam. In the Lancashire region of the CRS the Haslingden branch is the only one remaining, with the forty members continuing to meet every fortnight. However, the CRS is still committed to the Guild in the north-west, giving Merseyside grants to enable Guild branches to send delegates to their annual congress.

The CWS Manchester Band, founded in 1901 as the Tobacco Factory Band, was part of the brass band tradition in the north. It took part in the major contests winning the National Championship twice (runner-up seven times) and the British Open four times (runner-up once). It recorded over 300 radio broadcasts, 150 titles on LP and made numerous TV appearances before it disbanded in the mid-1980s *(Co-operative Union)*.

Another loss since the Second World War has come about because of the selling of co-op property, so that many co-ops no longer possess separate premises or rooms for Member Relations activities. Certainly, the Burnley area of the CRS Lancashire Region conforms to this pattern, although some old co-op halls are still to be found on Merseyside, such as the Christopher and Laird Street halls, and the United Norwest has halls at Wythenshaw and Chorlton. The problem of obtaining suitable venues and meeting places has been exacerbated in recent years by the extended opening hours of co-op shops.

Nevertheless, the movement still aims to combine worthy causes with having fun. The Member Relations Department of United Norwest supports a wide range of cultural, sporting and leisure groups, many of which are reported on in the society's own newspaper, *Activity*. Groups include dance troupes, namely the Kaleidoscope Wheelchair and Able Bodied Dance Group at Radcliffe, dramatic and operatic societies, choirs, including the one at Oldham, and orchestras such as the Youth Steel Band Orchestra. In terms of sport, sponsorship is given to the Littleborough Rugby League Club, swimming teams and galas and to various bowling leagues and competitions, like the Bury Women's Tournament, besides a basketball club and cycling competition. For the less energetic there are camera clubs, painting classes, dress-making, knitting and an over sixties club.

The range of activities supported by the CRS is similar to that covered by the United Norwest. For example, the Co-operative Players, 'Olde Tyme' dances and a children's dancing school are to be found in the Merseyside region. In 1988–9 it gave a grant to a new arts organisation in Liverpool called the Communications Arts Trust. In the Lancashire region computer and photography clubs are organised at the Burnley Leo's Superstore, there is a mother and toddler group in Barnoldswick, and elsewhere there are personal growth workshops and children's dance groups.

Supplementing the regular social activities are a number of major annual events such as the CRS's Poetry Festival and the Young People's Film and Video Festival; the latter has been extended to include regional events, like the one on Merseyside. Similarly, a speech and drama festival is held at Bolton under the auspices of United Norwest. Another notable date in the co-operative calendar is May Day, with celebrations held in Burnley, Leigh and Manchester. The Burnley event, begun fifteen years ago in conjunction with the North-East Lancashire Trades Council, includes political speeches, marquees and

The first official May Day holiday was in 1978 and the following year the first 'May Day on Towneley Park', Burnley, took place. The CRS concentrated on the event as a family fun day. It is now an annual event and since the mid-1980s CRS has been joint sponsor with the Trades Council *(Jean Turnbull)*.

amusements. It has become a popular family day out and now constitutes by far the largest event with an estimated 18,000 people attending in 1993. The Co-operative movement still commemorates International Co-operators' Day on the first Saturday in July and United Norwest further marks the occasion with a special service in Manchester Cathedral. Some Lancashire co-operators still hold annual summer fêtes, such as the Wythenshaw's Members' Group. In honour of a former president of the then Manchester & Salford Society, United Norwest invites a prominent speaker to give the annual Walter Frost Memorial Lecture at one of Manchester's universities. Past speakers have included Glenys Kinnock and the late John Smith. Lancashire co-ops round off the year with special Christmas celebrations, such as the Burnley town centre entertainments organised by the CRS Lancashire Region together with the local Chamber of Commerce, and the family carol service complete with co-op choirs and brass bands held in Manchester Cathedral by the United Norwest.

Conclusion

Although the Co-op has had problems in adapting to the new business and social conditions of the post-war period, and disappeared from some parts of the country, it seems appropriate to end on a high note, stressing the continued emphasis on community involvement and social activities which are still very much alive and kicking in its traditional heartland of Lancashire. Despite the many changes in buying and selling habits and the centralising policies of the co-operative leadership, the co-ops of Lancashire have tried to retain their unique identities. Co-operative societies grew out of the community in which they were founded and were run by and for local people, becoming in many cases an integral part of the social fabric. As social changes continue to undermine much of the welfare provisions and community identity, there is still a need for institutions like the Co-op.

Appendix

In 1968 the Lancastria Co-op was formed by the amalgamation of Blackpool & Fleetwood, Lancaster & District and the Preston societies. By 1972 several other societies had been taken over, namely Windermere, Southport, Fylde and Carnforth, so that Lancastria extended from Windermere in the north to Formby on Merseyside in the south and east to Ingleton and Sedbergh. In 1976 Lancastria joined the Wigan & Bolton Co-op to create Greater Lancastria (Blackburn dropped out of earlier talks). On 22 May 1983 Greater Lancastria merged with North Midland to form United Co-operatives. Its trading area stretched from Lancashire in the north to Staffordshire in the south with stores in parts of Lancashire, Yorkshire, Cheshire, Derbyshire and Greater Manchester. During the 1980s a number of other co-ops came under United's wing, such as Eccles, Prestwich and Longridge in 1983, Blackburn in 1984, St Helens (Central Region) in 1985 and Warrington (Southern Region) in 1987.

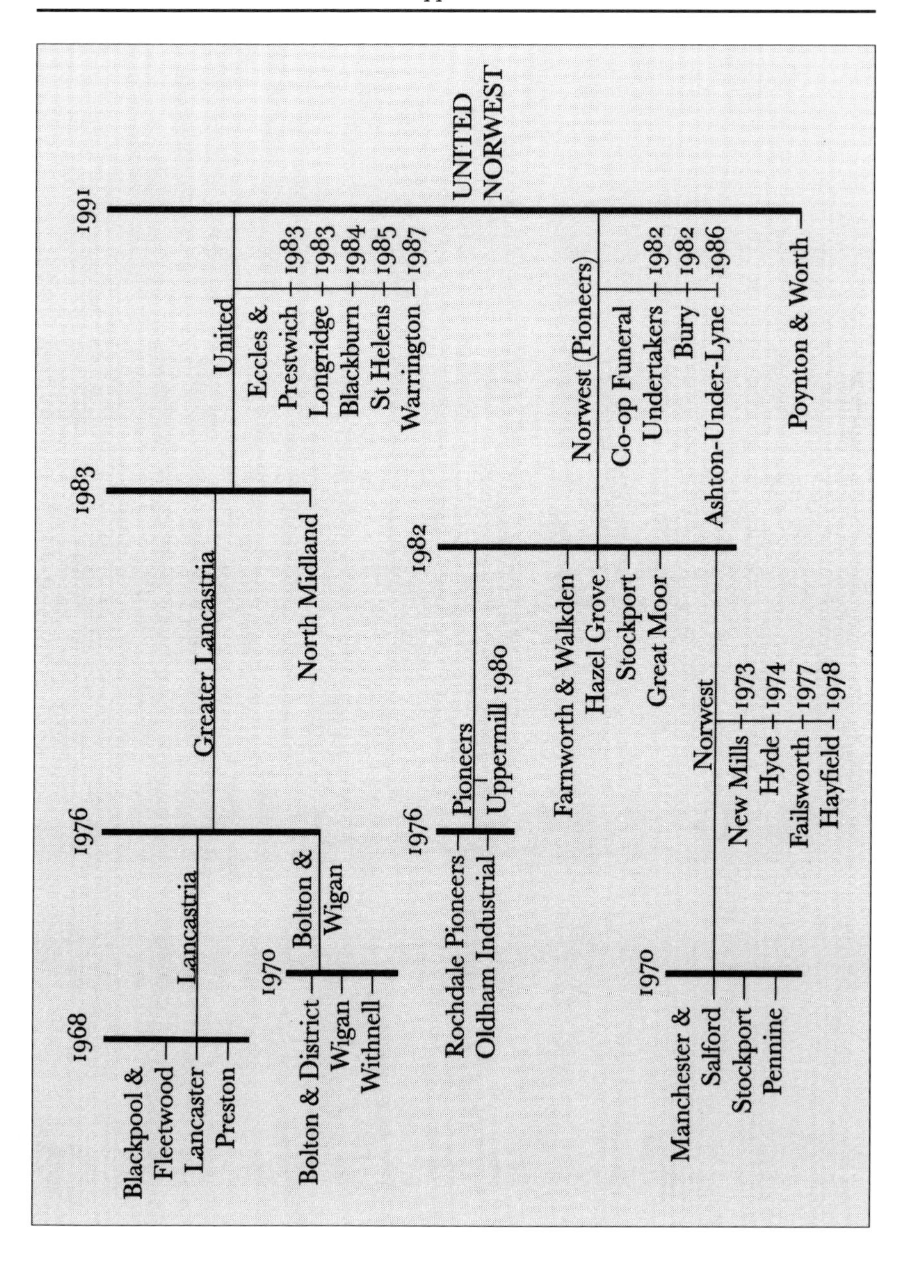
1968
1970
1976
1982
1983
1991
Blackpool & Fleetwood
Lancaster
Preston
Lancastria
Bolton & District
Wigan
Withnell
Bolton & Wigan
Greater Lancastria
North Midland
United
Eccles & Prestwich 1983
Longridge 1983
Blackburn 1984
St Helens 1985
Warrington 1987
UNITED NORWEST
Rochdale Pioneers
Oldham Industrial
Pioneers
Uppermill 1980
Farnworth & Walkden
Hazel Grove
Stockport
Great Moor
Norwest (Pioneers)
Co-op Funeral Undertakers 1982
Bury 1982
Ashton-Under-Lyne 1986
Poynton & Worth
Manchester & Salford
Stockport
Pennine
Norwest
New Mills 1973
Hyde 1974
Failsworth 1977
Hayfield 1978

Further Reading

Newspapers and Periodicals

The Co-operative News
The Producer
Women's Outlook
The Wheatsheaf

Co-operative Records

The Co-operative Directories: 1887, 1893, 1905, 1910, 1916, 1922, 1928, 1931, 1932, 1934, 1940, 1951, 1957, 1968, 1972.
The Co-operative Congress Reports
The Co-operative Statistics
The Co-operative Women's Guild Annual Reports
CRS Ltd., *Social Reports*: 1988, 1990, 1992.

Co-operative Society Records

Many societies in Lancashire produced their own publications, including jubilee and centenary histories, and some also had their own journals. These can be found in local libraries and record offices as well as the Co-operative Union Library in Manchester.

Books

Birchall, John, *Co-op: the People's Business* (Manchester, 1994).
Bonner, Arnold, *British Co-operation: the History, Principles and Organisation of the British Co-operative Movement* (Manchester, 1961).
Carr-Saunders, A. M., Sargant Florence, P. and Peers, Robert, *Consumers' Co-operation in Great Britain* (London, 1938).
Cole, G. D. H., *A Century of Co-operation* (Manchester, 1945).
Gaffin, Jean and Thoms, David, *Caring and Sharing: A Centenary History of the Co-operative Women's Guild* (Manchester, 1983).
Gosden, P. H. J. H., *Self Help: Voluntary Associations in the Nineteenth Century* (London, 1973).
Jefferys, James B., *Retail Trading in Britain 1850–1950* (Cambridge, 1954).

Davies, Margaret Llewelyn (ed.), *Life As We Have Known It, by Co-operative Working Women* (London, 1931 reprinted London, 1978).

Maternity: Letters from Working women (London, 1915 reprinted London, 1978).

Redfern, Percy, *The New History of the CWS* (Manchester, 1938).

Salt, Chrys and Wilson, Mervyn, *We Are Of One Blood: Memories of the First 60 Years of the Woodcraft Folk* (London, 1985).

Webb, Catherine, *The Woman With The Basket: The History of the Women's Co-operative Guild 1883–1927* (Manchester, 1927).

Articles

Pollard, Sidney, 'Nineteenth-Century Co-operation: from 'Community Building to Shopkeeping', in Asa Briggs and John Saville (eds.), *Essays in Labour History*, vol. 1 (London, 1967, 2nd edn.).

Pollard, Sidney, 'The Foundation of the Co-operative Party', in Asa Briggs and John Saville (eds.), *Essays in Labour History*, vol. 2 1886–1923 (London, 1971).

Purvis, Martin, 'The Development of Co-operative Retailing in England and Wales, 1851–1901: A Geographical Study', *Journal of Historical Geography*, vol. 16, no. 3, July 1990.

Theses

Alcock, Edwina, 'The Liverpool Co-operative Society, 1886–1939', University of Lancaster MA dissertation, 1986.

Angus, R. N. S., 'The Co-operative in Oldham, 1850–1950', University of Lancaster MA dissertation, 1979.

Claber, D. H., 'The Blackpool Industrial Co-operative Society, 1885–1910', University of Lancaster MA dissertation, 1991.

Clow, Ruth D., 'The Women's Co-operative Guild, 1906–1926: Co-operative Values and a Changing World', Manchester Polytechnic BA dissertation, 1981.

Laker, C. L., 'Co-operative Stores and Private Traders in Preston, 1870–1906', University of Lancaster MA dissertation, 1981.

Riding, D., 'Burnley Equitable Co-operative and Industrial Society, 1860–1914', University of Lancaster MA dissertation, 1983.

Smith, Jenny, 'The Co-op's Response to the Retailing Revolution: a Preston Case Study', Preston Polytechnic BA dissertation, 1986.

Southern, Jayne, 'The Co-operative Movement in the Inter-War Period: Cleator Moor, a Case Study', University of Lancaster MA dissertation, 1990.